Animals Growing Up

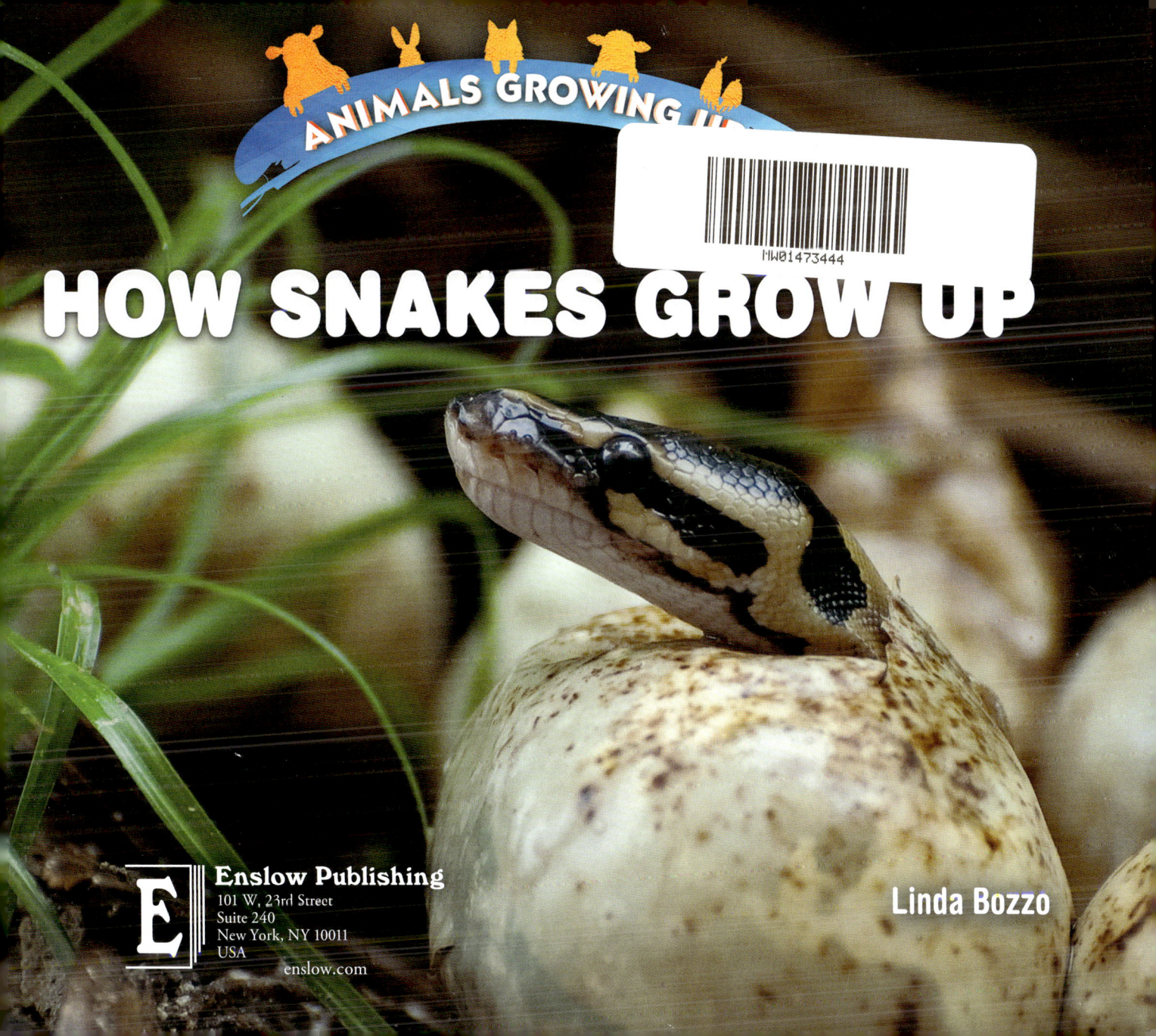

HOW SNAKES GROW UP

Enslow Publishing
101 W. 23rd Street
Suite 240
New York, NY 10011
USA
enslow.com

Linda Bozzo

WORDS TO KNOW

clutch A group of eggs laid at about the same time.

insects Small animals with six legs and a body with three parts that may also have wings.

predators Animals that kill and eat other animals to live.

prey An animal that is killed and eaten by another animal.

reptiles Animals that are cold blooded, usually lay eggs, and have a body covered with scales or hard parts like a shell.

shed To fall off.

snakelet A young snake.

species A group of the same kind of living thing that has the same scientific name.

venom Something an animal makes in its body that harms other animals.

CONTENTS

WORDS TO KNOW 2

HEY, BABY! 4

ON THEIR OWN 6

BABY SNAKES 8

SNAKES ATTACK 10

HUNTERS. 12

SNAKELETS SNACK 14

OPEN WIDE 16

SHEDDING SNAKELETS 18

STAY SAFE 20

SNAKES GROW. 22

LEARN MORE. 24

INDEX. 24

HEY, BABY!

Snakes are **reptiles**. Most **species**, or kinds, of snakes hatch from eggs. The mother snake lays a **clutch** of eggs. Other snakes are born live from their mothers.

FAST FACT

Snakes do not build nests for their eggs. They lay them in loose soil or sand.

A baby python hatches from its egg. Pythons grow up to be some of the largest snakes in the world.

ON THEIR OWN

Many mother snakes do not care for their young. The young snakes are left to live on their own. A young snake is known as a **snakelet**.

A green snakelet slithers along the forest floor.

FAST FACT

Pythons are snakes that stay with their eggs.

BABY SNAKES

The baby snakes' markings and coloring look the same as their parents'. Snakes can be brown, black, red, yellow, green, blue, or a mix of colors.

FAST FACT

Baby snakes are born with an egg tooth that will later fall off. The tooth helps them break out of the egg or the sac they are born in.

Baby corn snakes break out of their eggs.

SNAKES ATTACK

Snakes only attack when they are hungry or to protect themselves. Some snakes kill their **prey** before eating it. Others do not. Eating gives the snakelet the energy it needs to grow.

FAST FACT

Some snakes will use their venom to kill their prey. But not all snakes have venom.

A cobra snakelet raises the front part of its body off the ground when scared. It can spit venom at its attackers.

HUNTERS

Snakes are hunters. They must catch their prey in order to eat. Snakes use their tongues to pick up the scent of their prey. Snakelets can spend hours looking for food. Others wait for their prey to pass by.

FAST FACT

Some snakes wrap their bodies around their prey and squeeze them to death.

A diamondback rattlesnake flicks its forked tongue as it hunts. It kills its prey with venom.

SNAKELETS SNACK

Snakelets must learn to hunt for food on their own. Snakes eat meat. Snakelets snack on small animals such as frogs, lizards, mice, and **insects**.

FAST FACT

The size of the snake decides the size of its dinner! Larger snakes eat larger animals.

A bush viper snakelet has captured a frog to eat. This species of snake is only found in Africa.

OPEN WIDE

Snakes do not have the kind of teeth needed to chew their food. They have sharp fangs that point backward. Most snakes must swallow their prey whole.

FAST FACT

Snakes can open their mouths wider than their own body.

An eyelash viper snakelet stretches its mouth wide to swallow a lizard whole.

SHEDDING SNAKELETS

A snake's skin has thousands of scales. It doesn't grow as the snakelet gets bigger. Snakes must **shed** their skin as they grow. Young snakes grow quickly. Snakelets shed their skin several times a year.

A boa snakelet sheds its old skin tail first. Its tail end is shiny and colorful. The rest of its body is dull and cloudy from still being covered in old scales.

FAST FACT

A snake rubs its head on something rough to loosen the old skin so it can be shed.

STAY SAFE

Snakelets move around. They search for hiding places to stay safe. Snakelets are more likely to be attacked by **predators** than adult snakes. Birds are well-known for being predators of snakes.

FAST FACT

A weasel-like animal called a mongoose is famous for eating dangerous snakes. The mongoose is not hurt by venom.

A snakelet is an easy meal for a mongoose. The mongoose is fast and can move away from snake strikes. Its thick fur also protects it from bites.

SNAKES GROW

Snakes keep growing their entire lives. Large snakes usually live longer than small snakes. Snakes can live more than ten years in the wild. They can have their own babies at two to three years old.

The yellow anaconda can grow up to 15 feet (5 m) and weigh 77 pounds (35 kg)! It can live 15 to 20 years in nature.

FAST FACT

Snakes do not like the cold. There are no snakes living in Antarctica.

LEARN MORE

Books

Cider Mill Press. *Discovering Snakes Handbook.* Kennebunkport, ME: Applesauce Press, 2019.

Gish, Melissa. *Snakes.* Mankato, MN: Creative Education, 2017.

Weingarten, E. T. *I See a Snake.* New York: Gareth Stevens Publishing, 2019.

Websites

National Geographic Kids: Super Snakes
kids.nationalgeographic.com/explore/nature/super-snakes/
Find out eight awesome facts you might not already know about snakes.

San Diego Zoo Kids: Python
kids.sandiegozoo.org/animals/python
Learn about pythons, some of the largest snakes in the world!

INDEX

Africa, 15
boa, 19
bush viper, 15
cobra, 11
coloring, 8
corn snake, 9
eggs, 4, 5, 7, 9
egg tooth, 9
eyelash viper, 17
fangs, 16
food, 12, 14, 16
mother, 4, 6
mouth, 17
python, 5, 7
rattlesnake, 13
scales, 18, 19
size, 15
skin, 18, 19
tongues, 12, 13
yellow anaconda, 23

Published in 2020 by Enslow Publishing, LLC
101 W. 23rd Street, Suite 240, New York, NY 10011

Copyright © 2020 by Enslow Publishing, LLC.

All rights reserved.

No part of this book may be reproduced by any means without the written permission of the publisher.

Library of Congress Cataloging-in-Publication Data

Names: Bozzo, Linda, author.
Title: How snakes grow up / Linda Bozzo.
Description: New York : Enslow Publishing, 2020. | Series: Animals growing up | Audience: K to Grade 3. | Includes bibliographical references and index.
Identifiers: LCCN 2019008574| ISBN 9781978512474 (library bound) | ISBN 9781978512450 (paperback) | ISBN 9781978512467 (6 pack)
Subjects: LCSH: Snakes—Development—Juvenile literature. | Snakes—Infancy—Juvenile literature.
Classification: LCC QL666.O6 B739 2020 | DDC 597.96—dc23
LC record available at https://lccn.loc.gov/2019008574

Printed in the United States of America

To Our Readers: We have done our best to make sure all website addresses in this book were active and appropriate when we went to press. However, the author and the publisher have no control over and assume no liability for the material available on those websites or on any websites they may link to. Any comments or suggestions can be sent by email to customerservice@enslow.com.

Photos Credits: Cover, pp. 1, 5 Heiko Kiera/Shutterstock.com; interior pages 4-23 (background), pp. 13, 15, 17 Mark_Kostich/Shutterstock.com; p. 7 sarocha wangdee/Shutterstock.com; p. 9 Dan Olsen/Shutterstock.com; p. 11 Ali Bernie Bugaay Shutterstock.com; p. 19 Andrew Bee/Oxford Scientific/Getty Images; p. 21 Dave Hamman/Lonely Planet Images/Getty Images; p. 23 James Gerholdt/Photolibrary/Getty Images; back cover and additional interior pages background graphic 13Imagery/Shutterstock.com